OUR URBAN LEGACY
MEDIEVAL TOWNS

CLIFFORD B. MOLLER

HORIZON PRESS, N.Y.

ACKNOWLEDGEMENTS

For their invaluable help in the production of this book the author is indebted to:

Gabriele E. Cromie, for assistance in research, writing, editing, and photo layouts.

Mary E. Moller, for assistance in composition, writing and editing.

David, Catherine, and Jonathan Moller, for their help in locating many of the photographic subjects.

James R. Vaseff, for his photographs of;

Rothenburg ob der Tauber	pgs. 89–93
Überlingen,	pgs. 95–97
Neuchâtel,	pgs. 117, 119–121
Murten,	pgs. 132–133
Brugg,	pgs. 142, 143

CONTENTS

INTRODUCTION

When we walk through and experience the streets and squares of towns that had their origins, or were flourishing, in the Medieval Period, we are almost invariably struck by their charm. Strange to say, however, in our age of specialization, it is difficult to understand the beauty, the sense of harmony and of unity, that these towns convey. There is often no "style," and no imprint of a master-planner that we can identify.

For the most part, medieval towns and cities were not "designed." Their buildings and spaces are a reflection of the communal life of the period, which in turn was itself conditioned by those physical spaces among which people passed their lives.

Those medieval towns which still exist intact, or in part, often present useful models of viable urban communities. The spatial conditions inherent in them, embodying variety, flexibility, and human scale, exemplify many of the components of a humane, healthful environment. It may be said that these spaces help to satisfy many human needs, both physical and psychological. In fact, the houses, streets, lanes and squares of the medieval town are a direct result of the everyday practical needs of their inhabitants. Narrow streets give shelter from the summer sun and the cold winds of winter. Small squares where streets converge are natural and convenient meeting places. They and the buildings among them reflect an organic evolutionary process spanning several centuries. The men who shaped them were guided by their practical common sense and their respect for the natural conditions of the land, on the one hand, and, on the other, by their instinctive concern for the needs of the community.

★　★　★

The period which we call "The Middle Ages," spanning roughly the years 500 to 1500 A.D., was a period of increasing urban activity, particularly from the tenth century onwards, when favorable economic conditions encouraged political freedom for the growing middle class. According to medievalist Henri Pirenne, "its urban economy is worthy of the Gothic architecture with which it is contemporary. It created from nothing a system of social legislation more complete than that of any other era, not excluding our own. By suppressing middlemen between seller and buyer, it ensured the advantages of a low cost of living to the bourgeoisie; it was merciless in hunting down fraud; it protected the worker from competition and exploitation, regulated his work and pay, looked after his health, provided for his apprenticeship, prevented female or child labor, and, at the same time, succeeded in reserving for the town the exclusive right of supplying the surrounding country districts with its products, and in finding distant outlets for its trade."[1]

The beginning of the fifth century, by which time the Germanic tribes had conquered all of the Roman provinces, saw the whole of Western Europe politically transformed. Towns existing in the fourth century generally survived those invasions, sustained by a lively trade that continued between the West and the East on the Mediterranean basin.

In Pirenne's view, it was the Islamic invasions in 640–732 which destroyed the commerce of ancient Europe, and put an end to the old Mediterranean commonwealth.

The fact that the Mediterranean now became a "Moslem lake" stifled trade in the area; European cities went into general decline and what little commerce there was consisted almost entirely in the marketing of local goods and produce. Moslem influence was beginning to diminish in some areas when the Vikings descended into middle Europe

[1] *Les Villes et les Institutions Urbaines du Moyen Age,* vol. 1, p. 481.

early in the ninth century; and in 859 they were raiding along the Mediterranean. They ranged throughout France, and within a forty-year period pillaged Paris three times and burned it twice. Finally around the year 1000 the continent became more stable politically. The Vikings and other raiding groups had to some extent become assimilated into the life of Europe.

The crusades to the Holy Land, which began in 1099, reopened trade with the East. At about the same time new agricultural methods increased food supplies, and, as the population grew, business, trade, and industry began to prosper. In the tenth and eleventh centuries much marginal land was reclaimed and new towns were founded throughout Europe. The ensuing commercial revival continued throughout the twelfth century, by the end of which the economy of Europe was transformed from a relatively immobile agrarian one to a more flexible economy based on trade and industry. The country became city oriented. The old Roman cities were rejuvenated, and military burgs became predominantly mercantile. Supported by trade with the East by way of Venice, and via Flanders with Scandinavia, Europe became a land of thriving cities.

During the years 1000 to 1500, as a result of growing commerce and improved communications, these cities became the centers of a relative political freedom, a process in which the merchants took the initiative and directed events. The middle class now became an established order of society. Serfs and peasants had the opportunity to become free and acquire property and social advance was common. This increased social mobility fostered an emphasis on individuality. But personal growth and freedom could only be maintained along with group and community cooperation: one nurtured and encouraged the other. Burghers now took oaths of obedience to municipal authority, and pledged to provide help of various kinds to any other burgher needing it. Thus a community of law developed within the boundaries of the city, which was now, in effect, a commune administered by a council. Strong associations of tradesmen and artisans, called guilds or corporations, were more than trade-protective organizations. They were brotherhoods closely concerned in the effective functioning of the entire community. Community responsibility, a willing adherence to the interests of the town, in turn reinforced each individual's sense of identiy and worth.

The buildings, streets, squares, gardens, and courts of medieval towns, and the ways in which they relate to each other, reflect these new personal freedoms based on communal cooperation. Public and private spaces were interwoven to form the fabric of the town. Private houses and courts were visually and physically connected to public courts and streets. And these public open spaces were in daily use, the scene of lively economic and social activity.

Some of the towns illustrated in this book had their origin in the Roman era, or earlier, while others were founded later. All have been in continuous use since the late-medieval period. As newer structures were required from time to time, new materials and syles were sometimes introduced, but in all the towns and city areas depicted here the characteristic medieval urban spatial clusters have remained essentially the same over the years.

★   ★   ★

The popular assumption, often fostered by guide books, that the architecture of the past consists mainly of castles, churches and other monumental buildings, is both erroneous and unfortunate. The many areas containing non-monumental structures (residential, commercial, agricultural, etc.) which remain from earlier periods are also rich in interest. These areas embody evidence about the daily life of the time when they were built, which helps to give meaning to the more famous "monuments." Architecture is not an abstract art whose productions are to be viewed as museum exhibits. It consists in the human structuring of space for human use; and all these man-made spaces, whenever and however they were shaped, were and are of great social significance to their users.

First, the structured environment is an important influence, direct and indirect, on the shaping of personality, and the choice, as well as the attainment of personal goals. Although this fact has received relatively little recognition, there is indeed a continuous interaction on the part of each individual with the interrelated spaces that make up a dwelling, a neighborhood, or a town, a continuous response to such phenomena as size, scale, proportion, openness, closure, light, and color.

There is also a role played by structured space in conditioning interpersonal and family relationships: whether or not, for example, the immediate living area affords convenient circulation patterns among individual spaces, whether it offers sufficient opportunities for privacy, for work, for conversations, and for solitary and shared pursuits.

In addition, the architectural environment affects people's lives, and thus their mental health, through its influence upon extra-familial contacts, patterns of community interaction and group association—in the fostering or inhibiting of casual meetings, the formation of friendships, and the regulation of group activities. Architecture, then, can be defined as "the dynamic interaction of space and personality. Neither structured space nor mankind has any meaningful existence independent of the total life situation of which both space and man are a part. They can be observed only as components within a system of interaction."[2] Viewed this way, medieval towns and cities can provide important insights for present-day and future environmental planning.

★　★　★

It becomes increasingly apparent that modern cities must, for the most part, be judged a failure as an environment for human beings. In spite of technological advances resulting in a greater degree of physical health and convenience, our newer urban centers cannot compare environmentally with the typical medieval towns.

Ironically, it is often *because* of our so-called "mastery" of nature, and our impressive technological achievements, that our cities have become increasingly unrelated to human needs. Serious frustrations are experienced daily by city dwellers in their effort to exist in a static, unyielding and hostile environment. Frequently in actual danger from machines, subject to extreme mechanical noise, to air pollution, and to overwhelming, out-of-scale structures amid a

[2]C. B. Moller, *Architectural Environment and Our Mental Health,* Horizon Press, 1968.

rigid monotony of grid-patterned streets, they are increasingly alienated both from nature and from other equally frustrated and irritable people. These frustrations accelerate the incidence of individual and social ills: expanding circles of anxiety, job failures, family disruptions, delinquency, and crime.

The physical spaces of modern towns both reflect and foster these ills. Most of our smaller towns have to a great degree lost whatever cohesive urban character they once had. Their main roadways are largely given over to what is known as strip-zoning—lined with bleak and treeless shopping centers, fast-food chain stores, service stations, and parking areas which are macadamized deserts. No place for the pedestrian here.

At the same time, builders in the larger cities, and in many so-called resort areas, are producing ever larger anti-human structures. The scale of these buildings, and the institutional aridity of their public interior spaces, constitute a negation of individual identity and dignity which every city-dweller has at some time felt, and many are able to articulate. The correspondingly grandiose exterior spaces, wherever they have been preserved and paved over to set off the structures, have little use. They are often inimical to practical human needs, such as protection from sun, wind and rain; and they leave unfulfilled the more subtle psychological needs: for a sense of spatial security, for relaxation of tension, and for social interaction. A preoccupation with "originality" frequently results in bizarre structural forms, whose static, self-contained spaces bear no relation to the surrounding areas. Such buildings are apt symbols of the personal alienation our society fosters.

Many areas of the modern city are really isolated, economically homogeneous ghettos, whose high-rise apartments occupy sites planned like typical suburban tracts, with socially meaningless external spaces. Dwellers here exist in identical badly-planned cells that usually give a mere illusion of privacy—whose arbitrary, unfunctional spaces only accentuate their users' growing suspicion that something is wrong, life has little meaning. Social contact is superficially experienced in dreary halls or barren parking garages and lots, whose spaces induce only tension and a desire for escape.

It is the ghetto-like character of these planned urban "neighborhoods" which provokes the most serious charge against them—their tendency to homogenize their residents, while isolating them from other areas and other groups within the city.

In other words, these structures and spaces, in sharp constrast to those of most medieval towns are unable to foster for their users either a sense of individual dignity or a sense of community.

★ ★ ★

In any final reckoning a successful society has to be based on a recognition of the importance of the individual, and of each individual as a link in a network of complex interpersonal and social relationships. If the physical, psychological and social needs of individuals are respected and satisfied, then the community can be a stable one, truly civilized, and fulfilling, for the individuals who belong to it.

It is precisely these universal human requirements that the typical spaces of medieval urban centers seem so well able to satisfy. The following photographs show that, in any over-all view of these areas no one element appears isolated from the rest; all are organically interrelated. Here, the individual is not dwarfed: buildings and the exterior spaces that unite them are in proportion to their human users. In private courtyards and gardens one can enjoy both a relation to nature and a sense of the urban community which is visible beyond. Small semi-public spaces, entrance courts, and terraces form comfortable transitions between private and public areas. There is a wide choice of interesting pedestrian ways from one area to another; and a wide variety of public spaces fosters easy communication and social interaction. Although, literally, each of these towns was made up of a collection of individual buildings, it can be seen that in essence each was one common structure. The streets of the town served as corridors and as extensions of the interior spaces, connecting the various rooms—individual dwellings, with public interior and exterior spaces. Individual houses, at the same time, retained their primary and multiple importance: one not only lived but worked at home. There were fashioned and fabricated the family's clothing and a great many objects of everyday household use; and there also, often, the family conducted its special handicraft or trade.

The streets were an important part of daily life. They were not only pedestrian corridors, but also places for the carrying on of trade, and the fabrication and marketing of goods. Shops displayed their wares there, sometimes under colorful awnings. Open spaces, where streets widened or intersected, served for larger markets, for the storage of goods and often for a watering place, where a fountain was placed either in the center, or, obeying the dictates of topography and circulation, to one side. Naturally, these communal spaces also served as sites for informal meetings, news-trading, and leisurely conversation. In the smaller exterior spaces adjacent to individual dwellings, the residents often placed chairs and benches, and would sit there in good weather, usually with some handwork which permitted sitting, watching and participating in the life of the community flowing about them. In those houses where a family's trade or craft was carried on were often set large barn-size doors, which, standing open during the day, could reveal the entire workshop of the blacksmith, woodworker, silversmith, leather-tanner, cooper, or wheelwright to the passers-by, and in turn permit these workers to share in the life of the street.

All this lively activity was carried on against a background of friendly noises: the sawing and hammering of the carpenters, the ring of the blacksmith's anvil, the rumble of carts, and the churchbells marking the hours. Morning, noon, and evening the Angelus was heard; bells pealed joyously for the feast days, and summoned all the people of the town for assemblies. In addition, one could also hear, periodically, the "crying" of the news, and special announcements, and finally, each night, the "all's well!" of the watchman making his rounds.

Many of these scenes and activities—the big open market, the open atelier, the neighbors seated outside their doorways, carving, tinkering, sewing, knitting, and chatting—can still be observed in those European towns of medieval origin whose spaces have remained unchanged into this century. Exploring within them, one can observe a spatial balance that seems to serve, rather than endanger, those basic needs for privacy and for social interaction which were discussed above. Both the buildings and the spaces around them seem to speak for a natural order of things, having evolved from the natural needs of the people who would inhabit them.

The houses, frequently located over shops or adjoining them, were built of thick masonry, stone or wood, which effectively shielded their residents from heat and cold, and to some extent from the daily noise. This could not have been obnoxious, in any case, since all was relatively quiet at night. Constructed from materials indigenous to the region, these solid medieval structures could effectively provide privacy, and at the same time, reinforce a relationship with the natural environment. Privacy, secured within the protective structure, could be found outside it as well, in the form of a private courtyard which completed many dwellings, and served naturally as an extension of one's house.

At the same time that the individual could easily seclude himself within the family from the populated world outside, he could as easily rejoin it. The fact that housing fell into comfortable clusters—combinations of private units which related to each other, and to the exterior spaces near them—encouraged pleasant social encounters. These groups of buildings, sharing common walls and common transitional spaces, formed optimum spatial relationships which served to encourage human relationships. This interplay between physical space and human personality, while probably not identified as such by those who built these medieval villages, was nevertheless a concept which was intuitively followed in the course of their construction.

The individual who lived in these surroundings inevitably experienced a sense of continuity, of belonging, and a sense of ease in neighborly communication and interaction. In short, despite the many physical dangers and discomforts he endured from limited medical knowledge and the threat of enemies outside the city walls, his basic relationship with his environment enhanced his daily life and contributed to a sense of fulfillment.

＊　＊　＊

A psychological condition that is widespread in today's urban environment is alienation, a condition characterized by serious doubts about self-identity, a loss of rapport with others, and a sense of meaninglessness. The spatial patterns typical of medieval towns undoubtedly helped, and may still help, to counteract these feelings.

Living in such a town one could hardly feel alienated. From one's window, a stimulating urban panorama presents itself. Many other roofs, windows, courts, terraces and gardens are in view, as well as streets and squares containing markets, shops, ateliers, and areas adaptable to a wide spectrum of uses. A few steps from one's door, it is possible to encounter a rich variety of human activities—people working at various trades, goods being sold and traded, intimate conversations and larger gatherings, different kinds of play. And even during the hours when this bustle of activity is suspended, the physical and aesthetic continuity of the spaces themselves, and the impression they convey of being, each and all, parts of a harmonious whole, are subtly at work to help the resident feel himself part of a community.

The spatial configuration of medieval towns offers a degree of variety and of choice which far exceeds any experienced in the typical modern town. This spatial variety is largely a result of the intermixing of workshops, market places, houses and other private and public buildings in the same general area. The fact that in the medieval period most people lived and worked in the same area was not only a practical convenience but doubtless an important factor in maintaining a sense of community. These people were less encumbered than we by the dichotomy, so widely felt in our time, between "life" and "work", with its implication that "work" is a necessary evil, or at least something apart from one's "real" life. Fewer such dislocations disrupted the natural flow of existence in the Middle Ages, and the urban areas which reflect this fact still encourage an intimate association of work and play with dwelling spaces.

Then as now the harmony of these towns' structures and spaces could contribute directly to the citizens' involvement in meaningful work. The sense of well-being that we believe was enhanced by this environment was not only reflected in the voluntary association of workers in their guilds, but is evidenced in the buildings and objects of all kinds which have survived to the present.

It has been said that the craftsmanship or art of the period has a simple strength derived from the artisans' strong sense of order, that each production—whether of "art" or of "craft," for practical use—exhibits a harmonious equilibrium among these elements: the form of the object, the material of which it was fashioned, and the ultimate use for which it was intended. In this context the word "use" can of course include the devotional aspects of much medieval painting and sculpture, as well as the aesthetic pleasure which they, and many other products, afforded and still afford. These works of craftsmanship, though often of anonymous origin, show always a great deal of individuality and originality, an individuality limited only by the necessities of intended use or of placement, and by the craftsman's respect for the character of his materials. Such things as the imaginative variations that we see in the shape and adornment of utensils, or in the rich pictorial illumination of beautifully lettered manuscripts—all these attest to the creative exuberance of their makers in this period.

When the spatial environment facilitates movement from individual seclusion to community involvement, and from familial privacy to productive work, so that all these situations and roles are felt to be meaningfully interrelated, then it can be said to foster creativity, responsibility, and individual fulfillment.

✳ ✳ ✳

In several ways, the typical medieval town also seems remarkably able to satisfy the basic human need for consistency, or order. The psychological concept of "consistency" describes a need to which all human beings are subject from earliest infancy, and which is apparent to thoughtful adults in the efforts they must make to adjust, both practically and emotionally, to the world around them. At all times we desire at least a minimum degree of order and comprehensibility in our environment; we need to have things "make sense." Acutely depressed individuals of any age will often describe the world around them as "meaningless," "confusing," or "making no sense," perceptions which ultimately have negative social consequences. In our century, it has become increasingly obvious that a disordered environment which seriously frustrates the basic human drive toward a rational consistency, can foster tension, emotional disorders and social disruption. What is now called "juvenile delinquency," for example, reflects the difficulty experienced by many adolescents in adjusting to an inhumane and bewildering physical environment; frequently they express their frustrations by spreading destruction and further chaos in the grim public housing complexes of our cities.

Since we are more accustomed to a rigid rectilinear urban plan, an overview of the typical medieval town may not immediately disclose its underlying order. Nevertheless, within these complex and seemingly casual clusters of streets and buildings, a consistent pattern does prevail—a pattern whose order, though subtle, is real and satisfying because it has evolved organically in response to human need and human use.

These interestingly varied streets do not curve or meander, narrow or widen accidentally or capriciously, as a result of someone's whim at a drawing board. Their pattern was imposed by the topography of the area, by the fact that they serve a number of community activities besides circulation, and by the logical relations among the structures and spaces which they connect. And the pattern, the spacing or clustering of these structures, and of the squares or other open areas formed by them, was itself governed by their respective functions and by the relations of these functions to one another: the relation of public to private, or residential to municipal, religious, commercial, and recreational.

Moreover, the buildings and the exterior spaces, whether larger or smaller and however varied in form, all have a "human scale." It is obvious that they were not intended to "impress," but effectively to serve their assigned functions. Their scale suggests that each is a logical unit in the total orderly organization of the town. Details such as doors, windows, stairs and arches reflect the size of their human users; and the streets are scaled to the needs of pedestrians and to the size of those vehicles appropriate for use within a densely organized urban complex. Finally, in these towns and villages, the sense of order is reinforced by the relative homogeneity of building materials, from easily identified local sources.

✶ ✶ ✶

Most medieval towns originally had walls built around them for protection against invaders. These also served (and, wherever they stand, still serve) to bind the town together as a physical and social unit. In many places individual dwellings, and occasionally a church or other building, were "built into," that is placed against, or in a corner of, the town wall. This, of course, together with the wall's outcropping towers, sentinel stations, and stairs, further accentuated that impression, which the medieval town still conveys, of one single, complex, but well-ordered structure.

At the same time, although these walls formed a sharp boundary between the urban area and the surrounding countryside, they did not isolate the residents of these towns from nature. On the contrary, the universal human need to feel part of and relate to the natural order of the physical world, to the flow and ebb of seasons, weather, winds, and the life of plants and animals, was effectively satisfied in the medieval town or village. The closeness of fields and woods, and the ease of access to them, necessarily made "nature" a part of everyone's everyday life. No haphazard diffusion of urban forms outside the walls—no sprawling suburbs—stood between the town and the encircling country, some of which was, and is, pastoral, and some quite wild. And the clever use of space within the city walls for plants and trees served and serves to form a series of links to the country. Venerable trees within the town's boundaries have been carefully nurtured over the years. Successive generations have improved this tie to nature by introducing more trees and shrubs wherever possible—in public squares and small parks, in private gardens, courts, and terraces, and even in some cases on roof-tops. Smaller spaces such as balconies, corners, stairs, and window boxes, have long been utilized for additional plants. And where some streets were widened in post-medieval times, trees were planted to form barriers between vehicles and pedestrians, and to temper the bleakness of parking areas. The tree-shaded country roads were echoed in the city's pleasant boulevards.

★ ★ ★

Thus far this discussion has focused on certain specific relationships between the structured spaces of medieval towns and the long-range psychological well-being of their inhabitants. There is yet another subtle quality, definitely and immediately felt in the towns illustrated here, and in many others surviving from that period—the quality which we loosely call "charm." It is interesting to observe how visitors from widely different backgrounds, and with otherwise disparate tastes, are affected by this quality. Almost without exception they respond with interest and delight to the experience of wandering through these urban spaces—no less in the tiny rural villages than in the older parts of major cities.

What is this nebulous "charm?" Medieval town-spaces, when first experienced in reality, or even through photographs, are a source of great pleasure. Is it entirely what we call "aesthetic pleasure," or something still more fundamental which perhaps involves an unconscious recognition of environmental values? What specific characteristics of the typical medieval town help to contribute to this pleasure? Some of them have already been touched on briefly in this essay. Our pleasure has to do, surely, with such things as texture and color, solidity, scale, irregularity, variety, and possibilities of choice. And we react positively to the evidence of care and continuity.

One of the more obvious visual aspects of these towns is their near-uniformity of color and texture. Structures of rough-hewn stone with slate roofs, and streets of round cobbles (grey or brownish, depending on the geology of the region), or structures of white plaster with red terracotta roofs, are satisfying to the eye, they appeal to our common craving for simplicity, naturalness and harmony. Where these are set off by the dark green of cypress or the brighter green of other trees, moss, and vines, one requires no other color contrasts. Here the pleasure is chiefly sensuous, involving a response to texture—directly experienced or imagined—no less than to form and color. But still another factor is operative in our response to the materials of which these towns are composed. Even if we are ignorant of their age, even if we mistake their origin by some centuries, we are immediately aware of their solidity and durability; in contrast to many modern structures, these medieval clusters impress us with an agreeable sense of permanence.

Another source of the pleasure which they afford is that quality of "human scale" which has already been cited as contributing to our impression of order. In the medieval town we immediately feel ourselves relating to our surroundings. A sense of rightness, or "fitness" (the town's spaces are literally fitted to our size), and ultimately a sense of "belonging" are the result. More specifically, the sequence of enclosed or semi-enclosed spaces that the town contains induces a subtle feeling of protection and security, while at the same time encouraging pleasant social encounters.

These urban spaces and structures reveal everywhere a loving attention to detail. One sees it in the structural details of buildings, such as entrances, corners, cornices, window embrasures, and balconies, and equally in public gardens, promenades, stairways, fountains—all carefully fashioned; and many residents have enhanced their dwellings with trees, flowers, vines, and with carefully chosen complementary materials.

Finally, because of all the qualities just described, and because of their age and the care with which they were originally put together, the spaces and structures within these towns are cherished. They are—nearly all of them, to a remarkable degree—kept clean. And they are *used,* there is little or no waste space. One of the chief lessons of these towns for our time is that density of population need not mean rigid uniformity and regimentation, nor chaos, nor squalor. For centuries many of these European towns and smaller cities have sustained a density which most American urban areas are only now approaching; and they have done so by means of a careful spatial economy combined with a determination not to sacrifice comfort.

✷ ✷ ✷

The concept of "variety" keeps coming up in these pages. Surely this is one of the most appealing features of the towns that have kept their medieval character. Because they were not "planned" to any significant degree, they are delightfully complex, and offer, alike to their residents and to the casual visitor, a truly remarkable variety of spatial experiences within even a small area. Although the town as a whole strikes one as coherent, as having a basic order, in the ways and for the reasons that I have discussed, there is no monotony. And implicit in the idea of variety, or complexity, is the idea of choice. In these towns and villages one is constantly able to choose, for example, among spaces of a comparable size but an astonishing variety of shapes, which are formed by the dictates of topography, by the meandering lanes, and by the clustering of structures which are themselves of a striking variety of shapes and sizes. And one can also choose between small, intimate, enclosed spaces (or narrow twisting streets) and areas which are larger, more open, even "grand" and "noble"—such as squares, plazas, terraces, the banks of streams and bridges, the battlements of the fortified towns, and often the exciting vertical spaciousness of multi-level streets connected by stairs.

Progressing through the medieval town, even one of those hillside or sea-cliff towns whose streets are extremely steep, one does not soon become tired. Interest, the pleasure derived from complexity, keeps fatigue away. There is always a "beyond" in view, always differing somewhat from the "here." The typical medieval town abounds in fascinating vistas: some long-range, of the surrounding country—farms, forests, sea, or mountains—and some very intimate, into the next street, over a small park or garden, up or down to another level. Often these vistas are framed by arches, integral parts of many structures from this period, which themselves occur in a rich variety of sizes and forms. Each newly-perceived space has an invitational quality—the stroller is eager to keep going.

The narrowness of most of these streets and lanes makes it necessary to move slowly; they enforce leisureliness. The first sentence of this essay begins, "When we *walk* through . . . the streets and squares of medieval towns. . . ." One cannot explore them in any vehicle at much more than a fast walking pace, and the words "saunter" or "stroll" best express the optimum way to experience their ever-changing, ever-inviting networks. It is when we walk, pause, and walk again that we perceive our environment most truly. When, strolling through a typical medieval town, or even leafing slowly through these photographs, we become aware of the whole town as a continuously unfolding sequence, we realize that the variety of spaces and their relationships with one another have qualities both of interest and coherence rarely found in any more recently planned urban environment.

The towns illustrated here are only representative of the many cities and towns of medieval origin that exist throughout Europe. Unfortunately in many instances their spaces and characteristics are rapidly being ruined by modern alterations. It is hoped that this book will inspire architects, planners, and the general public to enjoy, perhaps to aid in the preservation of, and above all to learn from these valuable urban legacies.

Sainte-Enimie
France

Located at one of the narrowest parts of the Gorge du Tarn, this village is on one of the ancient trails of Europe. Greek and Roman pottery has been found in this region. Sainte-Enimie derives its name from Princess Enimie, the daughter of Clotaire II. Legend states that at the end of the sixth century the princess was cured of leprosy when she bathed in the spring of "Burle." Grateful for this "miracle," she built a monastery there and the village developed around its walls.

During the Middle Ages the village was an active commercial center, noted for its hand-weaving, a trade carried on until mechanical looms became common in larger cities.

Farming, almond, walnut and cherry trees, the breeding of sheep and goats, and, of course, tourism, are its main sources of livelihood today.

La Malène
France

La Malène clings to the cliffs of the Gorge du Tarn, which forms the southern edge of "les Causses," a region of chalk plateaus to the South of the "Massif Central." There is evidence that cave dwellers, Troglodytes, lived in this area. In the sixth century a fortified monastery existed on the site of the village, and undoubtedly the descendants of the cave dwellers clustered around this monastery and originated the village. The monks, who were called "pioneer monks," built walls on the hillsides to maintain a few small arable plots, locally known as "bancels." Many of the small houses which were built into the side of the cliff are still in use today. These houses with their stone walls and terraces remind one of the cliff dwellings of the Pueblo Indians.

La Malène is located on a natural trail from Languedoc to the mountains of Aubrac, and was used by large sheep herds during their fall and spring migrations. Sheepherding, farming, and fishing in the Tarn, seem to have provided the residents of La Malène with a relatively comfortable existence.

Haute-Rive
France

Haute-Rive is located on the left bank of the river Tarn, about midway between Sainte-Enimie and La Malène.

A small and ancient farming village, it presents a fine example of the grouping of individual buildings, and the relationship of materials and spaces, so that the whole village has the quality of being one homogeneous structure.

Riquewihr
France

Historical documentation refers to Riquewihr as early as 1094, and local tombstones indicate that the area was inhabited even earlier. The exterior walls and ramparts were built in 1291. It was occupied and pillaged during the "War of the Peasants" and during the Thirty Years War. After centuries under various rulers Riquewihr finally became French following the Peace Treaty of Lunéville in 1801.

The medieval aura of this town has been well preserved in its houses, fountains, towers and ramparts. It is surrounded by gentle, rolling country, vineyards and fir and chestnut tree forests. A walk through the vineyards on the northern hills offers an impressive view over the town's rooftops and turrets. Wines produced here were well known during the Middle Ages, and in 1575 an official decree prohibited the planting of inferior vines. An engraving by Merian from the year 1643 of the Schoenenberg (a mountain with many vineyards) bears the inscription "the Schoenenberg, where the noblest wine of this land is grown."

Colmar
France

Colmar, one of the loveliest towns in Alsace, has a long and colorful history, with a documented existence reaching back to the year 823.

Once part of the Carolingian Empire, it later came under the control of the House of Habsburg. It was annexed to France by Louis XIV in 1673, handed over to Germany in 1871 by the Treaty of Frankfurt, and finally returned to France in 1918.

"Maison Pfister," built in 1537, in the medieval section of the town, has been called one of the most beautiful houses in the world. It is one of many painted and beautifully sculptured houses, each with a distinct personality of its own.

The painter Martin Schöngauer lived and worked here during the fifteenth century, and his exquisite "Madonna of the Rose Arbor" is housed in the Church of Saint Martin, built during the thirteenth century. Another famous work of art, the Isenheim altarpiece by Mathias Grünewald, together with numerous other masterpieces of the Rhenish school of the fifteenth century, is in Colmar at the cloisters of the "Unterlinden" Museum, a thirteenth century Dominican convent.

Colmar continues its tradition as a center for the production of Alsace wine, Munster cheese, textiles, brewing and printing.

48-51

Saint-Jean-de-Buèges
France

This ancient village and its neighbor Pégairolles-de-Buèges, lie in a fertile valley surrounded by barren mountains. An unusual mountain spring and its crystal clear pool are the source of the stream (la Buège) that flows through the valley nurturing its crops.

Off the well-traveled tourist routes, these towns seem to have been bypassed by modern times. Although not economically prosperous, they exist tranquilly, in harmony with their peaceful surroundings, much as they have for hundreds of years.

52–57

Pégairolles-de-Buèges
France

Located in the Valley de la Buèges, and 4 kilometers from Saint-Jean-de-Buèges this very old and quiet village is nestled against the foot of a small rocky mountain and overlooked by the ruins of its ancient castle. The strength that lies in its communal, and organic, structure seems to have sustained the village throughout the centuries. One hardly notices the deterioration of some individual buildings.

58–61

Montpellier
France

An interesting, and venerable city, Montpellier was founded by the Romans, probably as a military outpost. Located at the narrowest passage of the Languedoc corridor, it became a natural converging point for the pilgrims, scholars, and merchants using that trading route.

In the tenth century and later in the Middle Ages, the town prospered as a fief of the counts of Toulouse, gaining fame for its spices imported from the East. By 1349, when Philip VI of France purchased it from the Kings of Majorca, who had controlled it since the thirteenth century, Montpellier had become a center of learning as well. The oldest medical school in Europe was founded here in 1180, and from the twelfth century onwards it has formed the nucleus of a major university.

Today Montpellier is the commercial, educational, and cultural center of the Languedoc region. It is a pleasure to arrive in the old center of this town, where many of the medieval spaces are still intact—all the more so since they are in sharp contrast to the dehumanizing apartments and other buildings that have recently been built on the outskirts.

62-65

Les Baux
France

Resembling an abstract rock sculpture built for human habitation, Les Baux has an illustrious and complex history. Excavated bones, jewelry and pottery are evidence that man has lived on the rocks of Les Baux since the Stone Age.

In the tenth century a powerful provincial family gained control of the land around the "rock," building their castle and ramparts there and rapidly gaining political power. For a time, one was king of Arles (1215). The political life of Les Baux was very active, with frequent alliances and conflicts from that time until 1481, when its fortresses and walls were knocked down by order of King Louis XI. In the sixteenth century a building renaissance took place under Anne de Montmorency. The castle was renovated and mansions built, but in 1631 much of the town was again destroyed in the reign of Louis XIII.

Today the village remains a decaying but interesting and beautiful example of ancient habitation.

66–73

Longuiers
France

The buildings, storage vaults, and fences of Longuiers, a very small farming village on a plateau about 20 kms. from the city of Millau, are constructed almost entirely of regional stones, so that at first sight it resembles a complex group of natural rocks blending with the surrounding plain.

Records and deeds from the archives of Millau, dating back to the thirteenth century, indicate that, from a very early single farm, Longuiers developed in the fourteenth century into a village owned by about ten resident farmers. Although constantly inhabited, it seems to have incurred few changes during the ensuing centuries. Stepping into its unpaved streets and viewing its enduring and harmonious clusters of buildings, one senses the continuity of the community from the thirteenth century up to the present.

74–79

La Couvertoirade
France

The village of La Couvertoirade, now occupied by a few shepherds, farmers and artisans, was once a stronghold of the religious order called the Knights Templar. The village is known to have been in existence prior to the twelfth century because it is mentioned in a papal bull of 1135. The Templars became lords of the village in 1181 and constructed the fortified walls and castle soon after.

Located in the southeast corner of the department of Aveyron, this village stands strangely alone, surrounded by partially wild country. The surrounding fields and woods and the village are largely untouched by modern times, and seem much the same as they were in the Middle Ages.

Rothenburg ob der Tauber
Germany

Still protected by its ramparts, Rothenburg occupies a commanding site in one of the bends of the river Tauber. It is one of the oldest towns along the "Romantic Road" which links the rivers Main and Rhine with the Bavarian Alps.

The area around Rothenburg is said to have been settled by the Celts as early as 500 BC. It is certain, however, that from the twelfth century onwards a castle stood on the plateau above the river, and that the town was then very small. It became larger in the thirteenth century and a town wall was erected during the years 1350–1380. By the year 1400 Rothenburg had approximately 6000 inhabitants. The present population is only about 12,500.

Rothenburg commemorates an event from the Thirty Years War (1618–1648) in a famous annual pageant. It is called the "Meistertrunk" (A magisterial bumper of wine). When the town was conquered by the imperial army under General Tilly, who threatened to destroy it, the general was offered a cup of the best local wine. He agreed to spare the town if a prominent citizen would empty in one draught a 6 pint (3½ liter) tankard of the same wine. The mayor, Georg Nusch, accomplished this feat, and the town remains to this day with its medieval charm virtually unaltered.

88–93

Überlingen
Germany

A biography of Saint Gallus mentions that he was called to the royal court at Überlingen in the early part of the seventh century to heal the duke's daughter. This is the first written reference to the town, which probably originated even earlier.

Around the year 1180, Frederic I "Barbarossa" started to plan the expansion of the town, building moats and walls to provide protection when crossing Lake Constance. Überlingen's prosperity in medieval times was based on mill trade, wine and grain, which permitted it to play an important role among the towns located along Lake Constance. The carved wood great hall of the town hall is a reminder of the town's wealth in those days. During the Thirty Years War Überlingen turned back the Swedish invaders in 1653, a victory commemorated in the annual "Sweden procession." The town was repeatedly conquered, however, and occupied between 1643 and 1649. These wars seriously affected its economic strength, especially the wine-growing business, and Überlingen never fully recovered.

The picturesque character of this town and its location on the shores of Lake Constance make it a very pleasant place to visit in Southern Germany.

Sintra
Portugal

Sintra is located on the slopes of the "Serra de Sintra" among three of the range's highest peaks. The contrast of granite mountains, lush, almost tropical vegetation, and the rugged Atlantic coastline below creates a beautiful and imposing scene.

The district has been inhabited since the days of the Romans, and possibly before, and several Roman tablets and funeral urns have been found here. Sintra was once a flourishing Moorish city; and among the legacy of the Moors is the castle, its oldest surviving building. It was built between 700 and 900 AD and looms over the town from one of the peaks, about 1400 feet above sea level. The town was recaptured from the Moors in 1147 by Alfonso I.

Portuguese royalty chose this beautiful town as their summer residence until as late as the nineteenth century, building an elaborate castle, the famous Royal Palace, and two magnificent botanical gardens. Sintra has inspired poets, among them Lord Byron, who called it "this glorious Eden."

This region, Colares, is noted for marble quarries, orange groves, and vineyards. Trade documents from the Age of Exploration indicate that Colares wine was a favorite on ships bound for India.

Castelo de Vide
Portugal

Situated near the border of Spain, this ancient town was settled by the Celts, conquered by the Romans in 44 AD, destroyed by the Vandals, and later occupied by the Arabs.

Partially surrounded by the Sierra Mamede mountains, and about 600 meters above sea level, Castelo de Vide has mineral springs, a gentle climate and lush forests of chestnut, oak and pine.

Many squares and streets have been unchanged since the fifteen and sixteenth centuries; these are to be found especially in the upper parts of town, where the following photographs were taken. The nucleus of the town is here, where the whitewashed houses, stepped high up the hillside, cluster around the foot of the castle, which was built in 1299. The small lanes are brilliant with flowers. Gothic arches, beautiful fountains, and ornate wrought iron work on windows and doors enhance the medieval character of the town.

The fountain depicted on the following pages is a good expression of the pace of the village at the time it was built. It has a roof for shelter, and even seats below it, making it a pleasant place to chat while getting the vital water supply.

102-107

Marvão
Portugal

Marvão, another ancient Portuguese border town close to Castelo de Vide in the same mountain range, was once a Roman outpost known as Herminio Minor. Its fortifications, built primarily to ward off attacks by the aggressive kings of Castile, were deemed impregnable during medieval times. The town was, in fact, not captured until the civil war, when the liberals took it by surprise in 1833.

Today Marvão is still largely enclosed by its great walls. The road leading to the town circles around the rocky spur on which it stands, and the village appears perched on the crest of the hill.

Small alleys gay with flowers wind up and down the hill, often through archways. High above the town stands the castle, which was built at the end of the thirteenth century. The colorful texture of the stone-paved streets, the tiled roofs, and the abundance of flowers, set off by the whitewashed houses, evokes in the visitor a feeling of happiness and contentment, that one feels must also be present in the everyday lives of the villagers, most of whom are olive and wine growers.

108–111

La Neuveville
Switzerland

The area on the shores of Lake Bienne now occupied by La Neuveville has been settled since the Stone Age. There the people known as "lake dwellers" constructed their grass huts, supported by wooden platforms and posts sunk into the lake. Narrow wood bridges connected them to the shore.

During the first century AD Roman settlers sent by Nero occupied this territory. In the fourth century Norsemen pillaged and burned the existing settlement, and only a few fishermen and shepherds lived there in the following years. Thick fir tree forests covered the area, and it became known as the "black valley." From the fifth century onwards the area was largely settled by Burgundians who fashioned their dwellings of native stone.

The town proper came into existence in 1312, when the archbishop of Basle purchased for a "barrel of silver" the allegiance of the local settlers and the right to build a fortified city.

This new town, Neuveville, became known as a "privileged town," because of the many rights and privileges extended to the citizens by the local lords who needed their support.

Neuchâtel
Switzerland

The pale ochre houses of Neuchâtel were described by Alexandre Dumas as being "carved out of a block of butter." Located on the hilly shore of Lake Neuchâtel and flanked by vineyards, the site is a most enticing point from which to see the entire range of the Middle Alps, including the majestic Mont Blanc.

The name Neuchâtel is derived from the "new castle" which formed the nucleus of the town in the fifth century. In the year 1011 the town, which was then not much more than a small fortified village, was given by King Rudolph III of Burgundy to his wife in a deed of gift. After the king's death in 1034, the town became part of the Holy Roman Empire, then went through a succession of rulers of various dynasties, becoming the property of a French family by inheritance in 1657. To celebrate the event, the new French ruler had 1,300 gallons of the local red wine poured into the Fountain of the Griffin which still exists today. In the year 1707, still by inheritance, Neuchâtel became the property of the first King of Prussia, and in 1815 it joined the Swiss Confederation. The King of Prussia finally acknowledged the town's independence in 1857.

Neuchâtel has always been a highly developed cultural center and its university enjoys a fine reputation.

116-121

Estavayer-le-Lac
Switzerland

An old town which owes its name to the Gallo-Roman nobleman Stavius, Estavayer-le-Lac was originally built along the shores of Lake Neuchâtel. As it grew houses spread up the hillsides and ultimately they were protected by a city wall.

The town was governed by three noblemen in the eleventh century, ruled by a Count of Savoy in the thirteenth century, and occupied by the citizens of Fribourg and Berne, in 1475, during the Burgundian wars. It formed an alliance with Fribourg during the time of the Reformation in 1536.

Much of its medieval legacy can still be enjoyed in Estavayer-le-Lac. There are ramparts and gate towers, arcades, old houses and a moated castle. The old engraving illustrated here depicts the town in 1599.

Some of the ancient customs survive among the town's 3,800 present-day inhabitants. Groups of children still go from house to house singing in celebration of the return of spring on the first day of May; men walk through the streets during Easter night singing the Surrexit; and the benediction of the boats of the Noble Guild of Fishermen takes place in August.

122–125

Fribourg
Switzerland

The house of Zähringen founded this town about 1178, choosing the location on the rocky cliffs of the Sarine river for its secure military position. Having survived many local wars, the town was admitted into the Swiss Confederation as a sovereign canton in 1481.

Many of the ancient Gothic houses are well preserved in the old quarter around the cathedral. These houses, the quaint fountains and wandering streets help preserve the aura of medieval times. On market days many of the citizens wear the traditional Swiss national dress.

The farms around Fribourg produce home-cured hams, bacon, sausage and cheese. Vacherin, a creamy cheese, is made in Alpine pastures during the summer and preserved in cherrywood boxes.

Murten
Switzerland

This small medieval town is located in the Swiss Midlands, on a gentle slope by the lake which bears its name.

Although there were settlements and fortifications in the immediate vicinity of Murten as early as 515 AD, the town proper was not established until about 1150 by a duke of Zähringen. It has been involved in many local wars, its most famous military involvement occurring in 1476, when the Duke of Burgundy, Charles the Bold, was defeated there by the Swiss Confederate Army. This victory is annually celebrated by a youth festival.

The original town wall was built in 1238 and then extensively repaired and enlarged in the fifteenth century. In 1488 a wooden protective roof and walkway were added and the wall has remained essentially unchanged since then. Today one can walk along the ramparts and gain fine views of the clustering roofs of the old town. As one can see in the etching of 1642 by Mathias Merian, and in the following photographs, the wall was, and is, an integral part of the town structure.

130–133

Murten.

Der See.

Aarau
Switzerland

The land that today is Switzerland was mostly colo-
nized by the Romans in the first century BC and later
invaded by the Barbarians. In the early Middle Ages the
Germanic Holy Roman Empire was the dominating political force. The decline of this Empire allowed feudal fami-
lies—Zähringen, Savoy, Kyburg and Habsburg—to gain
territorial strength and establish strongholds which developed into towns.

Aarau was one of these strongholds, founded about
1240 by the Kyburgs. Located on the rocky banks above
the river Aare, it is known locally as the town of gables
and gardens.

Today the town is the capital of the prosperous canton
of Aargau, where textile and machine industries flourish.
Although it has largely succumbed to modern expansion,
many of the spatial configurations formed by building clusters and courts retain their medieval heritage.

134–139

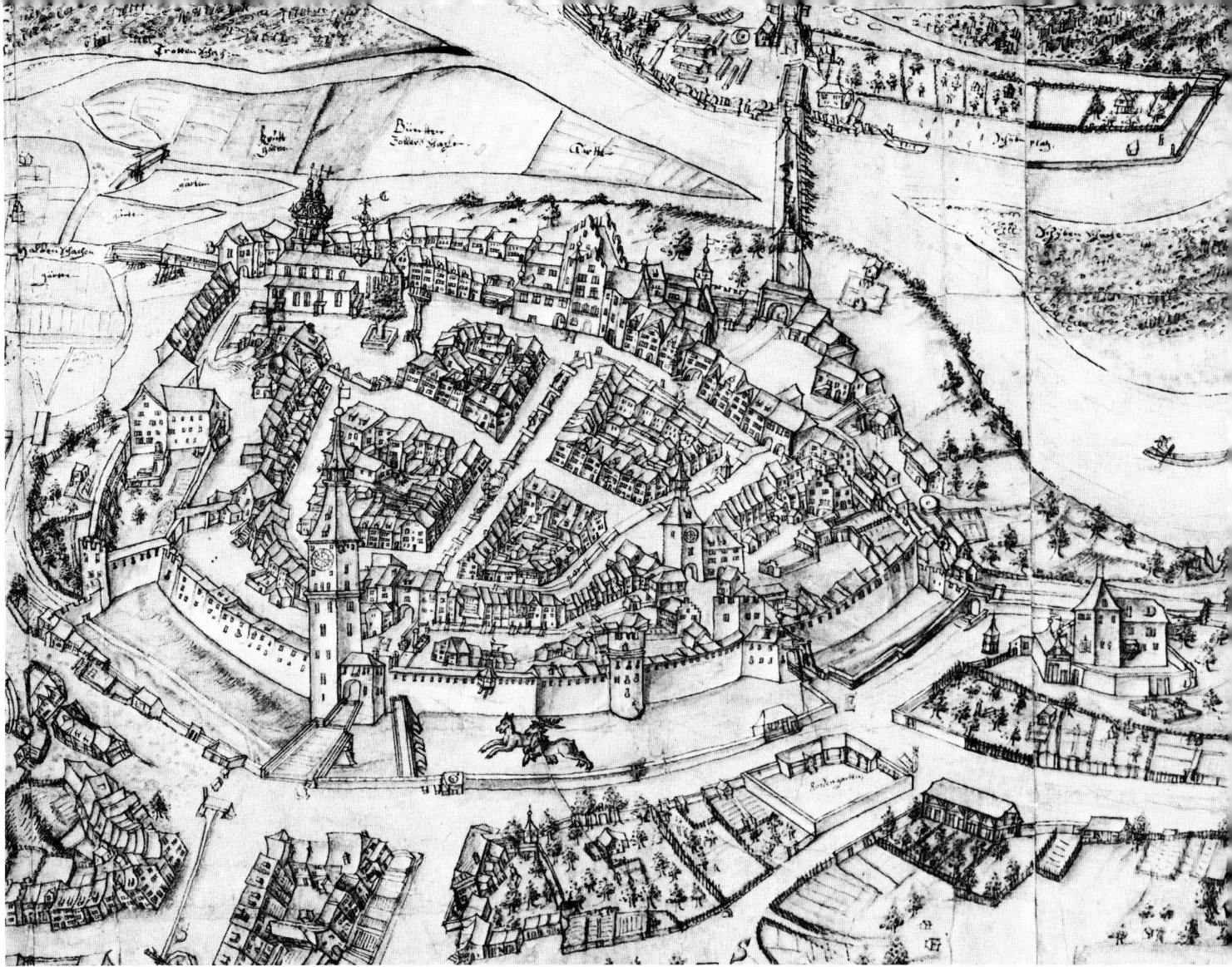

Halbenschattengarten

Blumen
Sollerswngen

Trotte

Halbenschattengarten

Rosengarten

Brugg
Switzerland

An old bridge town of 6,500 residents, Brugg is located in the so-called "Rübiland" (carrot country), one of the most fertile areas in Switzerland, where 95 percent of the land is cultivated.

Situated at the confluence of the rivers Aare, Reuss and Limmat, it has been a river crossing point since Roman times. The local museum houses an extensive collection of Roman artifacts, which were found at the Roman camp, Vindonissa, near Brugg.

As can be seen from the print of 1630, and the following photographs, the watch tower and the houses along the river have not changed much in three centuries. The town wall and the houses blend together and form a harmonious entity.

Brügg  **Im Aergaw.**

1630

Windisch

Königsfelden Closter.

Thun
Switzerland

Archeological explorations show that man has lived in
the area of Thun since at least 2000 BC. It was a fortified
Celtic settlement from 1000 BC to 15 BC, when it became
a Roman outpost, remaining so until 450 AD. The name
"Thun" is probably derived from the Celtic word "dun,"
meaning a fortified place, and may be the origin of the
word "town."

Thun was granted independence by the Counts of Kyburg in 1264; the document of independence, which consists
of four large sheets of parchment with many seals, is kept
in the town archives. In 1384 Thun was acquired by Berne
for 20,100 gold pieces. During the fifteenth century, trade
and commerce were blossoming, guild houses were built,
and the castle and the town walls were enlarged.

One of the many interesting features of the old town
is its main street, with two levels for pedestrians, arcades
at ground level and terraces above which serve as footpaths
and entrances to further shops and restaurants. They are
usually beautifully decorated with flowers, and the pedestrian is protected by broad overhanging roofs above. From
this level, an unusual covered staircase leads to houses
above, the church and the castle.

144–149

Porrentruy
Switzerland

The origins of Porrentruy are not clearly documented, but it is believed that the town existed as a settlement in Celtic and Roman times. The name "Pruntrut" first occurred in a document dated 1140, and by then the town must have been of some importance.

It seems that as early as the thirteenth century Porrentruy had strong walls and gates, since the town resisted a six week siege in 1283. Records show that the "grey bishop" of Basle called upon King Rudolph of Habsburg for help against Thierry de Montbéliard during that siege.

By the sixteenth century Porrentruy was a thriving and wealthy community. Many fine Gothic houses still exist from that period. Today the town is known principally for watch manufacturing and its excellent watchmaking school.

150–153

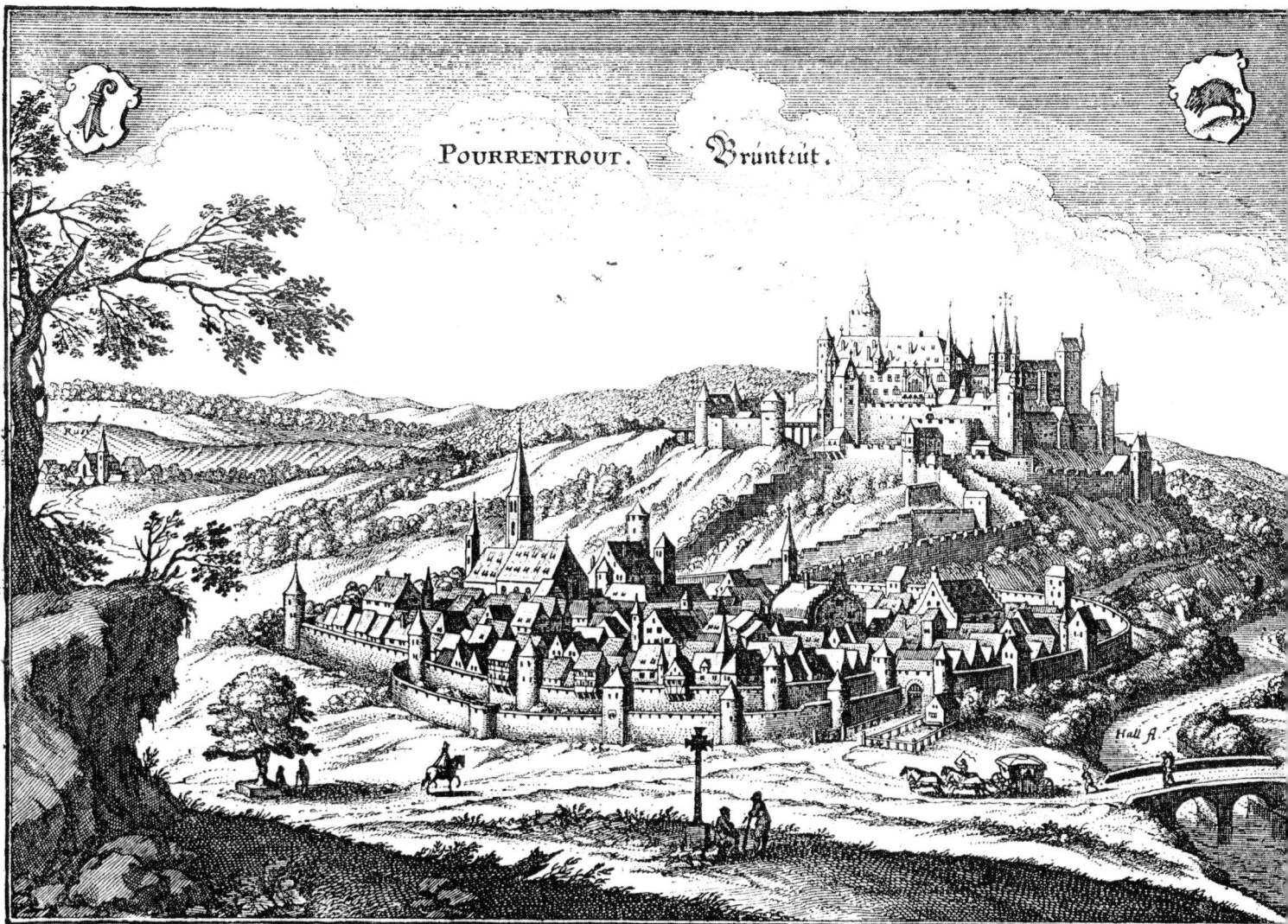

POURRENTROUT. Bruntrut.

Saint-Ursanne
Switzerland

Now a small bustling town of watchmakers, Saint-Ursanne was founded at the end of the sixth century. The hermit Ursicinus, a disciple of St. Colomba, died near the banks of the river Doubs at the site of the present town. His tomb was discovered about 635 by a pilgrim named Wandrille, who established a small monastic community there. The disciples organized themselves into an abbey under the Benedictine order, and the town grew up around the abbey and along the riverbank.

In the twelfth century, the settlement was enclosed by a semicircular wall from the mountain to the river. Though this wall and much of the town were destroyed by fire in 1403 and subsequent rebuilding has enlarged the town, it is still possible to trace the outline of the old wall. The gates of the town were rebuilt during the sixteenth and seventeenth centuries on the sites of the original medieval ones. These surviving gates, and the adjoining houses built into and on the site of the old wall, largely define the periphery of the old town; an area of houses with arched entrances, oriels, steeply pointed tiled roofs, wrought iron gates, and lively fountains.

The wooden bridge, depicted in the drawing of Saint-Ursanne of 1530, was replaced in 1728 by a four-arched stone bridge across which one enters the town today.

154–157

Saint-Ursanne *vers 1580.*

Nach einer Federzeichnung in Christian worelisers landschaftlichen Wappenbuch.

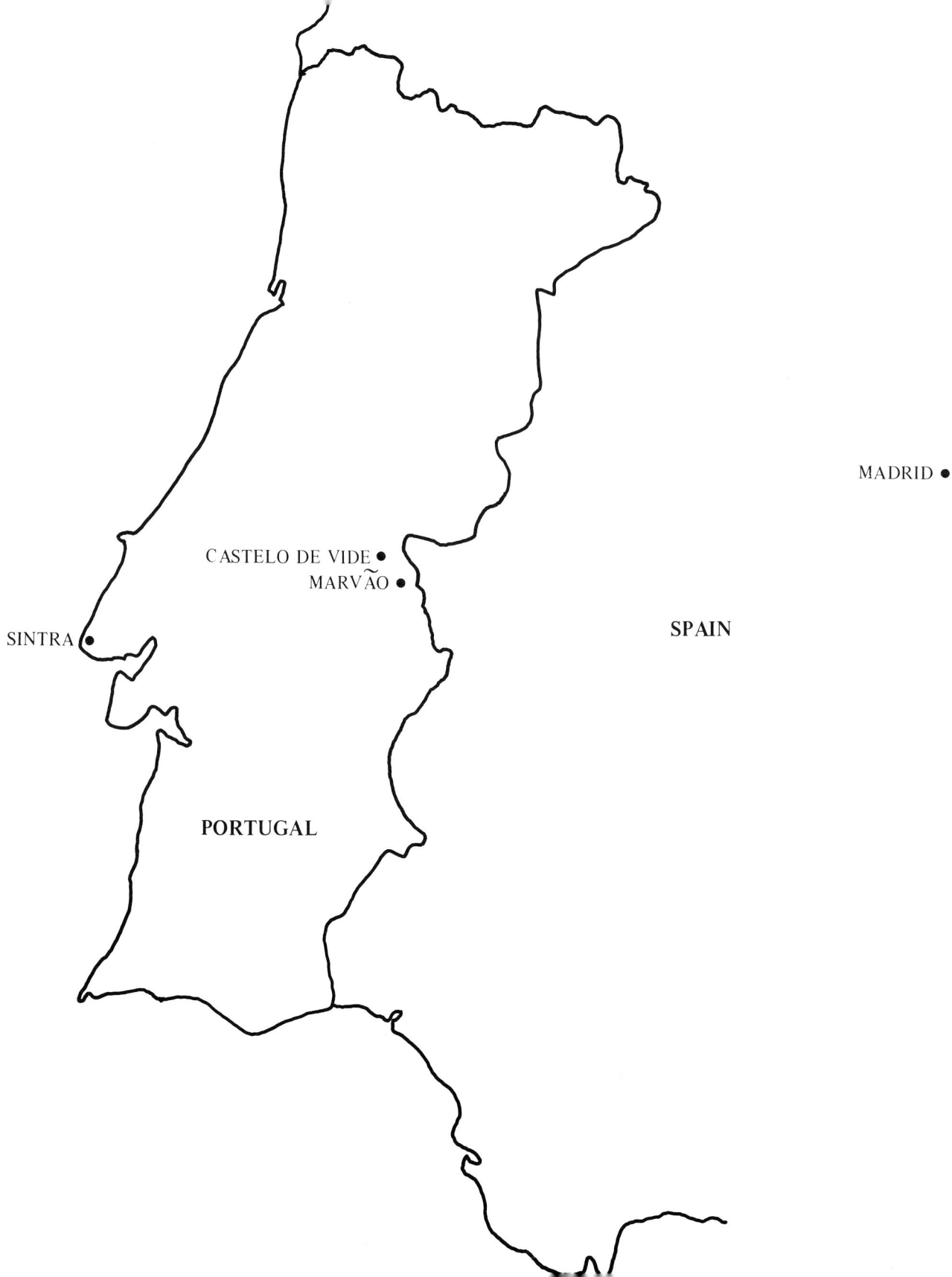

MADRID ●

CASTELO DE VIDE ●
MARVÃO ●

SINTRA ●

SPAIN

PORTUGAL

ROTHENBURG ●

GERMANY

PARIS

RIQUEWIHR ●

COLMAR ●

UBERLINGEN ●

PORRENTRUY ●
ST. URSANNE ●

BRUGG ●
AARAU ●

LA NEUVILLE ●
NEUCHÂTEL ●
ESTAVAYER LE LAC ●

MURTEN ●

FRIBOURG ● THUN ●

SWITZERLAND

FRANCE

ITALY

● STE ENIMIE
LA MALÈNE ● ● HAUTE RIVE

LONGUIERS ●
LA COUVERTOIRADE ● ● ST JEAN DE BUÈGES
● PÉGAIROLLES-de-BUÈGES

MONTPELLIER ●

● LES BAUX

0   50
MILES